J
385.22
Las

Lassieur, Allison.

Passenger trains.

$18.60

DATE		

Passenger Trains

by Allison Lassieur

Consultants:
Leslie Dean and Paul Kutta
Library Volunteers
National Railway Historical Society

Bridgestone Books

an imprint of Capstone Press
Mankato, Minnesota

Bridgestone Books are published by Capstone Press
818 North Willow Street, Mankato, Minnesota 56001
http://www.capstone-press.com

Library of Congress Cataloging-in-Publication Data
Lassieur, Allison.
    Passenger trains/by Allison Lassieur.
    p. cm.—(The transportation library)
    Includes bibliographical references and index.
    Summary: Discusses passenger trains, how they work, their history and inventors,
how modern trains compare to early models, and what it is like to travel on them.
    ISBN 0-7368-0363-7
    1. Railroads—Trains—Juvenile literature. 2. Railroads—History—Juvenile
literature. 3. Railroads—Passenger-cars—Juvenile literature. [1. Railroads.
2. Railroads—Trains.] I. Title. II. Series.
TF 148.L37 2000
385'.22—DC21   99-14632
                                                                      CIP

Editorial Credits
Rebecca Glaser, editor; Timothy Halldin, cover designer and illustrator;
    Heather Kindseth, illustrator; Kimberly Danger, photo researcher

Photo Credits
Amtrak, cover
Archive Photos, 16
Corbis, 14–15
Corbis/J.C. Grabill, 12–13
International Stock/Mike J. Howell, 18–19
James P. Rowan, 6
Marshall Smith, 8 (top right)
Photophile/Gary Conaughton, 4; Tom Tracy, 20
Unicorn Stock Photos/Jeff Greenberg, 8 (top left), 8 (bottom left);
    James L. Fly, 8 (bottom right)

Table of Contents

Passenger Trains 5

Traveling by Passenger Train 7

Passenger Train Cars. 9

How a Train Works 11

Before the Passenger Train 13

The First Trains 15

Early Passenger Trains 17

Passenger Trains around the World. 19

Passenger Train Facts 21

Hands On: Friction 22

Words to Know 23

Read More 24

Internet Sites 24

Index. 24

Passenger Trains

A train is a group of railroad cars pulled by a locomotive. A train travels on tracks. Some trains carry goods such as food or supplies. Passenger trains carry people between cities or across countries. Some passenger trains carry people to and from their jobs.

locomotive
the front car of a train; the locomotive holds the engine

Traveling by Passenger Train

Passengers buy tickets at ticket windows in train stations. Passenger trains pick up riders at train stations. Conductors take the tickets and help passengers board trains.

passenger
someone other than the driver
who travels by train or other vehicle

coach

sleeping car

dining car

lounge car

Passenger Train Cars

Most train passengers ride in coaches. These cars have rows of seats. On overnight trips, passengers may ride in sleeping cars. Sleeping cars have beds called berths. Passengers eat in the dining car. They watch the view through the large windows of the lounge car.

coach
a railroad car with rows of seats for passengers

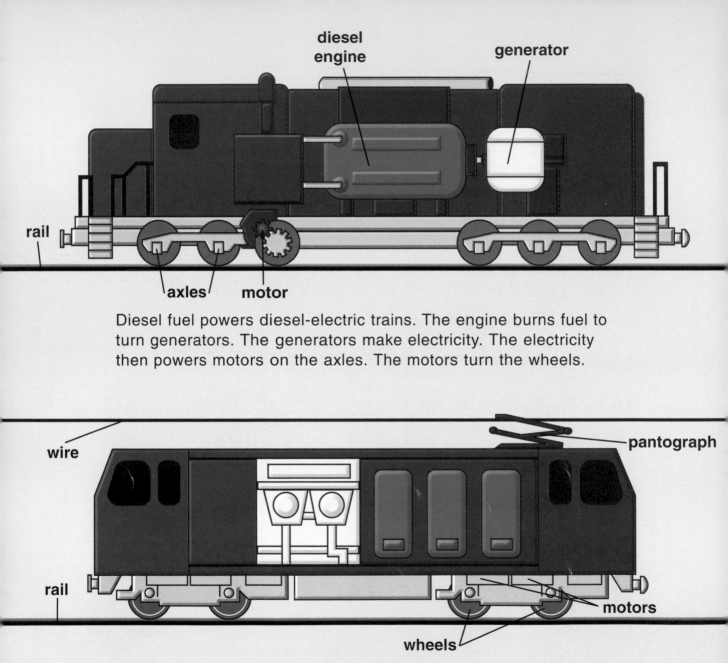

diesel engine

generator

rail

axles **motor**

Diesel fuel powers diesel-electric trains. The engine burns fuel to turn generators. The generators make electricity. The electricity then powers motors on the axles. The motors turn the wheels.

wire

pantograph

rail

motors

wheels

Electricity powers electric trains. The electricity comes from wires above the train. A pantograph connects the train to the wire. The electricity turns motors which turn the wheels.

How a Train Works

Diesel fuel and electricity are two power sources for train engines. The engine turns a train's wheels. The steel wheels ride on two smooth steel rails. Trains travel quickly because there is little friction between the wheels and rails.

friction

a force that slows down objects when they rub against each other

Before the Passenger Train

Before trains were invented, people traveled by boat or stagecoach. Boats on rivers and oceans carried people between cities. Horses pulled stagecoaches and wagons over land. But horses were slow. Trains could travel quickly over land.

stagecoach
a covered car with
seats pulled by horses

The First Trains

Trains were invented in England. In 1804, Richard Trevithick built the first steam locomotive that ran on tracks. It ran about 4 miles (6 kilometers) per hour. In 1829, George Stephenson built an improved steam engine called *Rocket*. It traveled 29 miles (47 kilometers) per hour.

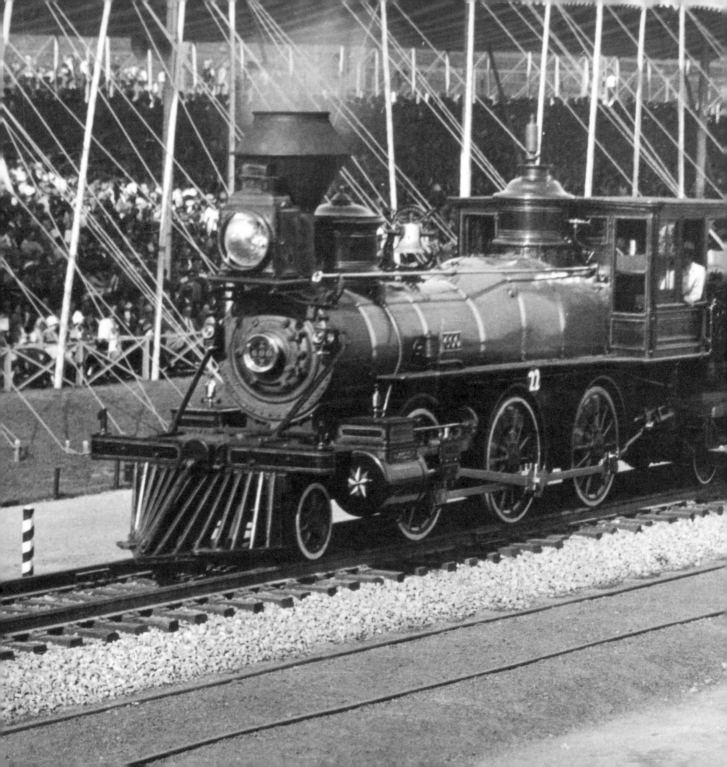

Early Passenger Trains

Steam locomotives pulled the first passenger trains. The first steam engines burned wood. Later models burned coal. These fuels polluted the air. Diesel fuel and electricity are cleaner than coal and wood.

pollute
to make something dirty or unsafe

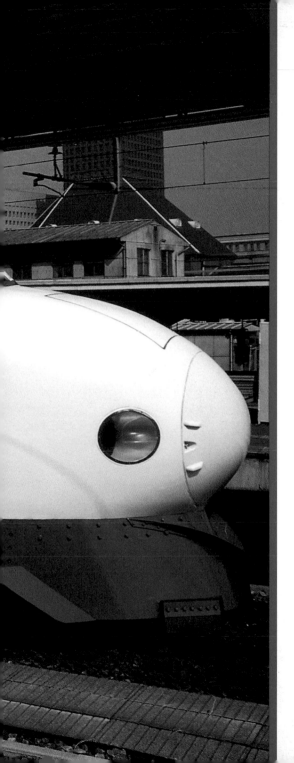

Passenger Trains around the World

Today, people in the United States travel most often by car or airplane. People in other countries more often ride passenger trains. Many of these countries have built fast trains. Japan, Germany, and France use high-speed electric trains.

Passenger Train Facts

- Grand Central Terminal in New York City is the largest train station in North America.

- The United States has more than 138,666 miles (223,155 kilometers) of train tracks. This is more than any country in the world.

- In 1990, the French TGV became the fastest train in the world. It traveled at 320 miles (515 kilometers) per hour in a test run. The TGV travels about 186 miles (300 kilometers) per hour on regular trips.

- Workers in Europe and Japan are testing maglev trains. Powerful magnets keep the trains four inches (10 centimeters) above the ground. This lowers friction and increases speed. Maglev trains are very expensive to build.

Hands On: Friction

Friction is a force that slows down objects when they rub against each other. You can see how friction works.

What You Need

A smooth board
A small toy car

What You Do

1. Push the car over a rough surface, such as dirt or grass. How far does the car roll before it slows down and stops?
2. Set the board on the ground. Push the car over the smooth board. How far does the car roll before it slows down and stops?

Friction will slow down the car on a rough surface. The car will travel farther on the board. There is less friction between the smooth board and the wheels. Trains travel quickly because there is not much friction between train wheels and rails.

Words to Know

berth (BURTH)—a bed in a train; some berths fold into seats.

diesel (DEE-zuhl)—a heavy fuel that burns to make power; many passenger trains run on diesel fuel.

electricity (ee-lek-TRISS-uh-tee)—a form of energy; electricity powers some passenger trains.

engine (EN-juhn)—a machine that makes the power needed to move something

generator (JEN-eh-ray-ter)—a machine that makes electricity

magnet (MAG-nit)—a piece of metal that has two ends called poles; the same poles push two magnets apart and different poles pull them together.

Read More

Morris, Neil. *Trains.* Traveling through Time. Parsippany, N.J.: Silver Burdett Press, 1998.

Richards, Jon. *Trains.* Cutaway. Brookfield, Conn.: Copper Beach Books, 1998.

Stille, Darlene R. *Trains.* A True Book. New York: Children's Press, 1997.

Internet Sites

B&O Railroad Museum
http://www.borail.org/
Steam Trains and Other Railroad Images
http://www.retroweb.com/steamtrains.html
Tina's Train Depot
http://www.dot.gov/edu/k5/depot.htm

Index

cities, 5, 13
coal, 17
diesel fuel, 10, 11, 17
electricity, 10, 11, 17
friction, 11
horses, 13, 21
rails, 11

stagecoaches, 13
steam engine, 15, 17
Stephenson, George, 15
tickets, 7
tracks, 5, 21
train station, 7, 21
Trevithick, Richard, 15